The Poetry of Bliss Carman

Volume XIV - Sappho: One Hundred Lyrics

"SAPPHO WHO BROKE OFF A FRAGMENT OF HER SOUL FOR US TO GUESS AT."

"SAPPHO, WITH THAT GLORIOLE
OF EBON HAIR ON CALMÈD BROWS—
O POET-WOMAN! NONE FORGOES
THE LEAP, ATTAINING THE REPOSE."
Elizabeth Barrett Browning

William Bliss Carman was born in Fredericton, in New Brunswick on April 15th 1861. He was educated at Fredericton Collegiate School before moving to the University of New Brunswick, obtaining his B.A. there in 1881. As is common with so many writers his first published piece was for the University magazine and for Carman that was in 1879.

After several years editing various magazines and periodicals Carman first published a poetry volume in 1893 with Low Tide on Grand Pré. There was no Canadian company prepared to publish and when an American company did so it went bankrupt.

The following year was decidedly better. His partnership with the American poet Richard Hovey had given birth to Songs of Vagabondia. It was an immediate success.

That success prompted the Boston firm, Stone & Kimball, to reissue Low Tide on Grand Pré and to hire Carman as the editor of its literary journal, The Chapbook.

Carman brought out, in 1895, Behind the Arras, a somewhat more serious and philosophical work centered on the premise of a long meditation, using the speaker's house and its many rooms, as a symbol of life and the choices to be made.

In 1896 Carman met Mrs Mary Perry King, who rapidly became patron, adviser and sometime lover. She also became his writing collaborator on two verse dramas.

In 1897 Carman published Ballad of Lost Haven, and in 1898, By the Aurelian Wall, the title poem itself was an elegy to John Keats and the book was a collection of formal elegies.

As the century turned Carman was hard at work on a five-volume set of poetry "Pans Pipes". The excellence of a number of these poems did much to install Carman as the most noted of Canadian Poets and eventually their own Poet Laureate.

In 1912 the final work in the Vagabondia series was published. Richard Hovey had died in 1900 and so this last work was purely Carman's. It has a distinct elegiac tone as if remembering the past works themselves.

On October 28th, 1921 Carman was honored by the newly-formed Canadian Authors' Association where he was crowned Canada's Poet Laureate with a wreath of maple leaves.

William Bliss Carman died of a brain hemorrhage at the age of 68 in New Canaan on the 8th June, 1929.

Index of Contents

INTRODUCTION

THE POETRY OF SAPPHO

If all the poets and all the lovers of poetry should be asked to name the most precious of the priceless things which time has wrung in tribute from the triumphs of human genius, the answer which would rush to every tongue would be "The Lost Poems of Sappho." These we know to have been jewels of a radiance so imperishable that the broken gleams of them still dazzle men's eyes, whether shining from the two small brilliants and the handful of star-dust which alone remain to us, or reflected merely from the adoration of those poets of old time who were so fortunate as to witness their full glory.

For about two thousand five hundred years Sappho has held her place as not only the supreme poet of her sex, but the chief lyrist of all lyrists. Every one who reads acknowledges her fame, concedes her supremacy; but to all except poets and Hellenists her name is a vague and uncomprehended splendour, rising secure above a persistent mist of misconception. In spite of all that is in these days being written about Sappho, it is perhaps not out of place now to inquire, in a few words, into the substance of this supremacy which towers so unassailably secure from what appear to be such shadowy foundations.

First, we have the witness of her contemporaries. Sappho was at the height of her career about six centuries before Christ, at a period when lyric poetry was peculiarly esteemed and cultivated at the centres of Greek life. Among the Molic peoples of the Isles, in particular, it had been carried to a high pitch of perfection, and its forms had become the subject of assiduous study. Its technique was exact, complex, extremely elaborate, minutely regulated; yet the essential fires of sincerity, spontaneity, imagination and passion were flaming with undiminished heat behind the fixed forms and restricted measures. The very metropolis of this lyric realm was Mitylene of Lesbos, where, amid the myrtle groves and temples, the sunlit silver of the fountains, the hyacinth gardens by a soft blue sea, Beauty and Love in their young warmth could fuse the most rigid forms to fluency. Here Sappho was the acknowledged queen of song—revered, studied, imitated, served, adored by a little court of attendants and disciples, loved and hymned by Alcaeus, and acclaimed by her fellow craftsmen throughout Greece as the wonder of her age. That all the tributes of her contemporaries show reverence not less for her personality than for her genius is sufficient answer to the calumnies with which the ribald jesters of that later period, the corrupt and shameless writers of Athenian comedy, strove to defile her fame. It is sufficient, also, to warrant our regarding the picturesque but scarcely dignified story of her vain pursuit of Phaon and her frenzied leap from the Cliff of Leucas as nothing more than a poetic myth, reminiscent, perhaps, of the myth of Aphrodite and Adonis—who is, indeed, called Phaon in some versions. The story is further discredited by the fact that we find no mention of it in Greek literature— even among those Attic comedians who would have clutched at it so eagerly and given it so gross a turn—till a date more than two hundred years after Sappho's death. It is a myth which has begotten some exquisite literature, both in prose and verse, from Ovid's famous epistle to Addison's gracious fantasy and some impassioned and imperishable dithyrambs of Mr. Swinburne; but one need not accept the story as a fact in order to appreciate the beauties which flowered out from its coloured unreality.

The applause of contemporaries, however, is not always justified by the verdict of after-times, and does not always secure an immortality of renown. The fame of Sappho has a more stable basis. Her work was in the world's possession for not far short of a thousand years—a thousand years of changing tastes, searching criticism, and familiar use. It had to endure the wear and tear of quotation, the commonizing touch of the school and the market-place. And under this test its glory grew ever more and more conspicuous. Through those thousand years poets and critics vied with one another in proclaiming her verse the one unmatched exemplar of lyric art. Such testimony, even though not a single fragment remained to us from which to judge her poetry for ourselves, might well convince us that the supremacy acknowledged by those who knew all the triumphs of the genius of old Greece was beyond the assault of any modern rival. We might safely accept the sustained judgment of a thousand years of Greece.

Fortunately for us, however, two small but incomparable odes and a few scintillating fragments have survived, quoted and handed down in the eulogies of critics and expositors. In these the wisest minds, the greatest poets, and the most inspired teachers of modern days have found justification for the unanimous verdict of antiquity. The tributes of Addison, Tennyson, and others, the throbbing paraphrases and ecstatic interpretations of Swinburne, are too well known to call for special comment in this brief note; but the concise summing up of her genius by Mr. Watts-Dunton in his remarkable essay on poetry is so convincing and illuminating that it seems to demand quotation here: "Never before these songs were sung, and never since did the human soul, in the grip of a fiery passion, utter a cry like hers; and, from the executive point of view, in directness, in lucidity, in that high, imperious verbal economy which only nature can teach the artist, she has no equal, and none worthy to take the place of second."

The poems of Sappho so mysteriously lost to us seem to have consisted of at least nine books of odes, together with epithalamia, epigrams, elegies, and monodies. Of the several theories which have been advanced to account for their disappearance, the most plausible seems to be that which represents them as having been burned at Byzantium in the year 380 Anno Domini, by command of Gregory Nazianzen, in order that his own poems might be studied in their stead and the morals of the people thereby improved. Of the efficacy of this act no means of judging has come down to us.

In recent years there has arisen a great body of literature upon the subject of Sappho, most of it the abstruse work of scholars writing for scholars. But the gist of it all, together with the minutest surviving fragment of her verse, has been made available to the general reader in English by Mr. Henry T.

Wharton, in whose altogether admirable little volume we find all that is known and the most apposite of all that has been said up to the present day about

"Love's priestess, mad with pain and joy of song,
Song's priestess, mad with joy and pain of love."

Perhaps the most perilous and the most alluring venture in the whole field of poetry is that which Mr. Carman has undertaken in attempting to give us in English verse those lost poems of Sappho of which fragments have survived. The task is obviously not one of translation or of paraphrasing, but of imaginative and, at the same time, interpretive construction. It is as if a sculptor of to-day were to set himself, with reverence, and trained craftsmanship, and studious familiarity with the spirit, technique, and atmosphere of his subject, to restore some statues of Polyclitus or Praxiteles of which he had but a broken arm, a foot, a knee, a finger upon which to build. Mr. Carman's method, apparently, has been to imagine each lost lyric as discovered, and then to translate it; for the indefinable flavour of the translation is maintained throughout, though accompanied by the fluidity and freedom of purely original work.

C.G.D. ROBERTS.

Now to Please My Little Friend

Now to please my little friend
I must make these notes of spring,
With the soft south-west wind in them
And the marsh notes of the frogs.

I must take a gold-bound pipe,
And outmatch the bubbling call
From the beechwoods in the sunlight,
From the meadows in the rain.

SAPPHO

I - Cyprus, Paphos, or Panormus

Cyprus, Paphos, or Panormus
May detain thee with their splendour
Of oblations on thine altars,
O imperial Aphrodite.

Yet do thou regard, with pity
For a nameless child of passion,
This small unfrequented valley
By the sea, O sea-born mother.

II - What Shall We Do, Cytherea?

What shall we do, Cytherea?
Lovely Adonis is dying.
Ah, but we mourn him!

Will he return when the Autumn
Purples the earth, and the sunlight
Sleeps in the vineyard?

Will he return when the Winter
Huddles the sheep, and Orion
Goes to his hunting?

Ah, but thy beauty, Adonis,
With the soft spring and the south wind,
Love and desire!

III - Power and Beauty and Knowledge

Power and beauty and knowledge,—
Pan, Aphrodite, or Hermes,—
Whom shall we life-loving mortals
Serve and be happy?

Lo now, your garlanded altars,
Are they not goodly with flowers?
Have ye not honour and pleasure
In lovely Lesbos?

Will ye not, therefore, a little
Hearten, impel, and inspire
One who adores, with a favour
Threefold in wonder?

IV - O Pan of the Evergreen Forest

O Pan of the evergreen forest,
Protector of herds in the meadows,
Helper of men at their toiling,—
Tillage and harvest and herding,—

How many times to frail mortals
Hast thou not hearkened!

Now even I come before thee
With oil and honey and wheat-bread,
Praying for strength and fulfilment
Of human longing, with purpose
Ever to keep thy great worship
Pure and undarkened.

O Hermes, master of knowledge,
Measure and number and rhythm,
Worker of wonders in metal,
Moulder of malleable music,
So often the giver of secret
Learning to mortals!

Now even I, a fond woman,
Frail and of small understanding,
Yet with unslakable yearning
Greatly desiring wisdom,
Come to the threshold of reason
And the bright portals.

And thou, sea-born Aphrodite,
In whose beneficent keeping
Earth, with her infinite beauty,
Colour and fashion and fragrance,
Glows like a flower with fervour
Where woods are vernal!

Touch with thy lips and enkindle
This moon-white delicate body,
Drench with the dew of enchantment
This mortal one, that I also
Grow to the measure of beauty
Fleet yet eternal.

V - O Aphrodite

O Aphrodite,
God-born and deathless,
Break not my spirit
With bitter anguish:
Thou wilful empress,
I pray thee, hither!

As once aforetime
Well thou didst hearken
To my voice far off,—
Listen, and leaving
Thy father's golden
House in yoked chariot,

Come, thy fleet sparrows
Beating the mid-air
Over the dark earth.
Suddenly near me,
Smiling, immortal,
Thy bright regard asked

What had befallen,—
Why I had called thee,—
What my mad heart then
Most was desiring.
"What fair thing wouldst thou
Lure now to love thee?

"Who wrongs thee, Sappho?
If now she flies thee,
Soon shall she follow;—
Scorning thy gifts now,
Soon be the giver;—
And a loth loved one

"Soon be the lover."
So even now, too,
Come and release me
From mordant love pain,
And all my heart's will
Help me accomplish!

VI - Peer of the Gods He Seems

Peer of the gods he seems,
Who in thy presence
Sits and hears close to him
Thy silver speech-tones
And lovely laughter.

Ah, but the heart flutters
Under my bosom,

When I behold thee
Even a moment;
Utterance leaves me;

My tongue is useless;
A subtle fire
Runs through my body;
My eyes are sightless,
And my ears ringing;

I flush with fever,
And a strong trembling
Lays hold upon me;
Paler than grass am I,
Half dead for madness.

Yet must I, greatly
Daring, adore thee,
As the adventurous
Sailor makes seaward
For the lost sky-line

And undiscovered
Fabulous islands,
Drawn by the lure of
Beauty and summer
And the sea's secret.

VII - The Cyprian Came to Thy Cradle

The Cyprian came to thy cradle,
When thou wast little and small,
And said to the nurse who rocked thee
"Fear not thou for the child:

"She shall be kindly favoured,
And fair and fashioned well,
As befits the Lesbian maidens
And those who are fated to love."

Hermes came to thy cradle,
Resourceful, sagacious, serene,
And said, "The girl must have knowledge,
To lend her freedom and poise.

Naught will avail her beauty,

If she have not wit beside.
She shall be Hermes' daughter,
Passing wise in her day."

Great Pan came to thy cradle,
With calm of the deepest hills,
And smiled, "They have forgotten
The veriest power of life.

"To kindle her shapely beauty,
And illumine her mind withal,
I give to the little person
The glowing and craving soul."

VIII - Aphrodite of the Foam

Aphrodite of the foam,
Who hast given all good gifts,
And made Sappho at thy will
Love so greatly and so much,

Ah, how comes it my frail heart
Is so fond of all things fair,
I can never choose between
Gorgo and Andromeda?

IX - Nay, but Always and Forever

Nay, but always and forever
Like the bending yellow grain,
Or quick water in a channel,
Is the heart of man.

Comes the unseen breath in power
Like a great wind from the sea,
And we bow before his coming,
Though we know not why.

X - Let There Be Garlands, Dica

Let there be garlands, Dica,
Around thy lovely hair.

And supple sprays of blossom
Twined by thy soft hands.

Whoso is crowned with flowers
Has favour with the gods,
Who have no kindly eyes
For the ungarlanded.

XI - When the Cretan Maidens

When the Cretan maidens
Dancing up the full moon
Round some fair new altar,
Trample the soft blossoms of fine grass,

There is mirth among them.
Aphrodite's children
Ask her benediction
On their bridals in the summer night.

XII - In a Dream I Spoke with the Cyprus-Born

In a dream I spoke with the Cyprus-born,
And said to her,
"Mother of beauty, mother of joy,
Why hast thou given to men

"This thing called love, like the ache of a wound
In beauty's, side,
To burn and throb and be quelled for an hour
And never wholly depart?"

And the daughter of Cyprus said to me,
"Child of the earth,
Behold, all things are born and attain,
But only as they desire,—-

"The sun that is strong, the gods that are wise,
The loving heart,
Deeds and knowledge and beauty and joy,—
But before all else was desire."

XIII - Sleep Thou in the Bosom

Sleep thou in the bosom
Of the tender comrade,
While the living water
Whispers in the well-run,
And the oleanders
Glimmer in the moonlight.

Soon, ah, soon the shy birds
Will be at their fluting,
And the morning planet
Rise above the garden;
For there is a measure
Set to all things mortal.

XIV - Hesperus, Bringing Together

Hesperus, bringing together
All that the morning star scattered,—

Sheep to be folded in twilight,
Children for mothers to fondle,—

Me too will bring to the dearest,
Tenderest breast in all Lesbos.

XV - In the Grey Olive-Grove a Small Brown Bird

In the grey olive-grove a small brown bird
Had built her nest and waited for the spring.
But who could tell the happy thought that came
To lodge beneath my scarlet tunic's fold?

All day long now is the green earth renewed
With the bright sea-wind and the yellow blossoms.
From the cool shade I hear the silver plash
Of the blown fountain at the garden's end.

XVI - In the Apple Boughs the Coolness

In the apple boughs the coolness

Murmurs, and the grey leaves flicker
Where sleep wanders.

In this garden all the hot noon
I await thy fluttering footfall
Through the twilight.

XVII - Pale Rose Leaves Have Fallen

Pale rose leaves have fallen
In the fountain water;
And soft reedy flute-notes
Pierce the sultry quiet.

But I wait and listen,
Till the trodden gravel
Tells me, all impatience,
It is Phaon's footstep.

XVIII - The Courtyard of Her House is Wide

The courtyard of her house is wide
And cool and still when day departs.
Only the rustle of leaves is there
And running water.

And then her mouth, more delicate
Than the frail wood-anemone,
Brushes my cheek, and deeper grow
The purple shadows.

XIX - There is a Medlar Tree

There is a medlar-tree
Growing in front of my lover's house,
And there all day
The wind makes a pleasant sound.

And when the evening comes,
We sit there together in the dusk,
And watch the stars
Appear in the quiet blue.

XX - I Behold Arcturus Going Westward

I behold Arcturus going westward
Down the crowded slope of night-dark azure,
While the Scorpion with red Antares
Trails along the sea-line to the southward.

From the ilex grove there comes soft laughter,—
My companions at their glad love-making,—
While that curly-headed boy from Naxos
With his jade flute marks the purple quiet.

XXI - Softly the First Step of Twilight

Softly the first step of twilight
Falls on the darkening dial,
One by one kindle the lights
In Mitylene.

Noises are hushed in the courtyard,
The busy day is departing,
Children are called from their games,—
Herds from their grazing.

And from the deep-shadowed angles
Comes the soft murmur of lovers,
Then through the quiet of dusk
Bright sudden laughter.

From the hushed street, through the portal,
Where soon my lover will enter,
Comes the pure strain of a flute
Tender with passion.

XXII - Once You Lay Upon my Bosom

Once you lay upon my bosom,
While the long blue-silver moonlight
Walked the plain, with that pure passion
All your own.

Now the moon is gone, the Pleiads
Gone, the dead of night is going;
Slips the hour, and on my bed
I lie alone.

I loved thee, Atthis, in the long ago,
When the great oleanders were in flower
In the broad herded meadows full of sun.
And we would often at the fall of dusk
Wander together by the silver stream,
When the soft grass-heads were all wet with dew,
And purple-misted in the fading light.
And joy I knew and sorrow at thy voice,
And the superb magnificence of love,—
The loneliness that saddens solitude,
And the sweet speech that makes it durable,—
The bitter longing and the keen desire,
The sweet companionship through quiet days
In the slow ample beauty of the world,
And the unutterable glad release
Within the temple of the holy night.
O Atthis, how I loved thee long ago
In that fair perished summer by the sea!

I shall be ever maiden,
If thou be not my lover,
And no man shall possess me
Henceforth and forever.

But thou alone shalt gather
This fragile flower of beauty,—
To crush and keep the fragrance
Like a holy incense.

Thou only shalt remember
This love of mine, or hallow
The coming years with gladness,
Calm and pride and passion.

XXV - It Was Summer When I Found You

It was summer when I found you
In the meadow long ago,—
And the golden vetch was growing
By the shore.

Did we falter when love took us
With a gust of great desire?
Does the barley bid the wind wait
In his course?

XXVI - I Recall Thy White Gown, Cinctured

I recall thy white gown, cinctured
With a linen belt, whereon
Violets were wrought, and scented
With strange perfumes out of Egypt.

And I know thy foot was covered
With fair Lydian broidered straps;
And the petals from a rose-tree
Fell within the marble basin.

XXVII - Lover, Art Thou of a Surety

Lover, art thou of a surety
Not a learner of the wood-god?
Has the madness of his music
Never touched thee?

Ah, thou dear and godlike mortal,
If Pan takes thee for his pupil,
Make me but another Syrinx
For that piping.

XXVIII - With Your Head Thrown Backward

With your head thrown backward
In my arm's safe hollow,
And your face all rosy

With the mounting fervour;

While the grave eyes greaten
With the wise new wonder,
Swimming in a love-mist
Like the haze of Autumn;

From that throat, the throbbing
Nightingale's for pleading,
Wayward, soft, and welling
Inarticulate love-notes,

Come the words that bubble
Up through broken laughter,
Sweeter than spring-water,
"Gods, I am so happy!"

XXIX - Ah, What Am I But a Torrent

Ah, what am I but a torrent,
Headstrong, impetuous, broken,
Like the spent clamour of waters
In the blue canyon?

Ah, what art thou but a fern-frond,
Wet with blown spray from the river,
Diffident, lovely, sequestered,
Frail on the rock-ledge?

Yet, are we not for one brief day,
While the sun sleeps on the mountain,
Wild-hearted lover and loved one,
Safe in Pan's keeping?

XXX - Love Shakes My Soul, Like a Mountain Wind

Love shakes my soul, like a mountain wind
Falling upon the trees,
When they are swayed and whitened and bowed
As the great gusts will.

I know why Daphne sped through the grove
When the bright god came by,
And shut herself in the laurel's heart

For her silent doom.

Love fills my heart, like my lover's breath
Filling the hollow flute,
Till the magic wood awakes and cries
With remembrance and joy.

Ah, timid Syrinx, do I not know
Thy tremor of sweet fear?
For a beautiful and imperious player
Is the lord of life.

XXXI - Love, Let the Wind Cry

Love, let the wind cry
On the dark mountain,
Bending the ash-trees
And the tall hemlocks,
With the great voice of
Thunderous legions,
How I adore thee.

Let the hoarse torrent
In the blue canyon,
Murmuring mightily
Out of the grey mist
Of primal chaos,
Cease not proclaiming
How I adore thee.

Let the long rhythm
Of crunching rollers,
Breaking and bellowing
On the white seaboard,
Titan and tireless,
Tell, while the world stands,
How I adore thee.

Love, let the clear call
Of the tree-cricket,
Frailest of creatures,
Green as the young grass,
Mark with his trilling
Resonant bell-note,
How I adore thee.

Let the glad lark-song
Over the meadow,
That melting lyric
Of molten silver,
Be for a signal
To listening mortals,
How I adore thee.

But more than all sounds,
Surer, serener,
Fuller with passion
And exultation,
Let the hushed whisper
In thine own heart say,
How I adore thee.

XXXII - Heart of Mine, if All the Altars

Heart of mine, if all the altars
Of the ages stood before me,
Not one pure enough nor sacred
Could I find to lay this white, white
Rose of love upon.

I who am not great enough to
Love thee with this mortal body
So impassionate with ardour,
But oh, not too small to worship
While the sun shall shine,—

I would build a fragrant temple
To thee, in the dark green forest,
Of red cedar and fine sandal,
And there love thee with sweet service
All my whole life long.

I would freshen it with flowers,
And the piney hill-wind through it
Should be sweetened with soft fervours
Of small prayers in gentle language
Thou wouldst smile to hear.

And a tinkling Eastern wind-bell,
With its fluttering inscription,
From the rafters with bronze music
Should retard the quiet fleeting

Of uncounted hours.

And my hero, while so human,
Should be even as the gods are,
In that shrine of utter gladness,
With the tranquil stars above it
And the sea below.

XXXIII - Never Yet, Love, in Earth's Lifetime

Never yet, love, in earth's lifetime,
Hath any cunningest minstrel
Told the one seventh of wisdom,
Ravishment, ecstasy, transport,
Hid in the hue of the hyacinth's
Purple in springtime.

Not in the lyre of Orpheus,
Not in the songs of Musaeus,
Lurked the unfathomed bewitchment
Wrought by the wind in the grasses,
Held by the rote of the sea-surf,
In early summer.

Only to exquisite lovers,
Fashioned for beauty's fulfilment,
Mated as rhythm to reed-stop
Whence the wild music is moulded,
Ever appears the full measure
Of the world's wonder.

XXXIV - "Who Was Atthis?" Men Shall Ask

"Who was Atthis?" men shall ask,
When the world is old, and time
Has accomplished without haste
The strange destiny of men.

Haply in that far-off age
One shall find these silver songs,
With their human freight, and guess
What a lover Sappho was.

XXXV - When the Great Pink Mallow

When the great pink mallow
Blossoms in the marshland,
Full of lazy summer
And soft hours,

Then I hear the summons
Not a mortal lover
Ever yet resisted,
Strange and far.

In the faint blue foothills,
Making magic music,
Pan is at his love-work
On the reeds.

I can guess the heart-stop,
Fall and lull and sequence,
Full of grief for Syrinx
Long ago.

Then the crowding madness,
Wild and keen and tender,
Trembles with the burden
Of great joy.

Nay, but well I follow,
All unskilled, that fluting.
Never yet was reed-nymph
Like to thee.

XXXVI - When I Pass Thy Door at Night

When I pass thy door at night
I a benediction breathe:
"Ye who have the sleeping world
In your care,

"Guard the linen sweet and cool,
Where a lovely golden head
With its dreams of mortal bliss
Slumbers now!"

XXXVII - Well I Found You in the Twilit Garden

Well I found you in the twilit garden,
Laid a lover's hand upon your shoulder,
And we both were made aware of loving
Past the reach of reason to unravel,
Or the much desiring heart to follow.

There we heard the breath among the grasses
And the gurgle of soft-running water,
Well contented with the spacious starlight,
The cool wind's touch and the deep blue distance,
Till the dawn came in with golden sandals.

XXXVIII - Will Not Men Remember Us

Will not men remember us
In the days to come hereafter,—
Thy warm-coloured loving beauty
And my love for thee?

Thou, the hyacinth that grows
By a quiet-running river;
I, the watery reflection
And the broken gleam.

XXXIX - I Grow Weary of the Foreign Cities

I grow weary of the foreign cities,
The sea travel and the stranger peoples.
Even the clear voice of hardy fortune
Dares me not as once on brave adventure.

For the heart of man must seek and wander,
Ask and question and discover knowledge;
Yet above all goodly things is wisdom,
And love greater than all understanding.

So, a mariner, I long for land-fall,—
When a darker purple on the sea-rim,
O'er the prow uplifted, shall be Lesbos
And the gleaming towers of Mitylene.

Ah, what detains thee, Phaon,
So long from Mitylene,
Where now thy restless lover
Wearies for thy coming?

A fever burns me, Phaon;
My knees quake on the threshold,
And all my strength is loosened,
Slack with disappointment.

But thou wilt come, my Phaon,
Back from the sea like morning,
To quench in golden gladness
The ache of parted lovers.

Phaon, O my lover,
What should so detain thee,

Now the wind comes walking
Through the leafy twilight?

All the plum-leaves quiver
With the coolth and darkness,

After their long patience
In consuming ardour.

And the moving grasses
Have relief; the dew-drench

Comes to quell the parching
Ache of noon they suffered.

I alone of all things
Fret with unsluiced fire.

And there is no quenching
In the night for Sappho,

Since her lover Phaon

Leaves her unrequited.

XLII - O Heart of Insatiable Longing

O heart of insatiable longing,
What spell, what enchantment allures thee
Over the rim of the world
With the sails of the sea-going ships?

And when the rose-petals are scattered
At dead of still noon on the grass-plot,
What means this passionate grief,—
This infinite ache of regret?

XLIII - Surely Somehow, in Some Measure

Surely somehow, in some measure,
There will be joy and fulfilment,—
Cease from this throb of desire,—
Even for Sappho!

Surely some fortunate hour
Phaon will come, and his beauty
Be spent like water to plenish
Need of that beauty!

Where is the breath of Poseidon,
Cool from the sea-floor with evening?
Why are Selene's white horses
So long arriving?

XLIV - O But My Delicate Lover

O but my delicate lover,
Is she not fair as the moonlight?
Is she not supple and strong
For hurried passion?

Has not the god of the green world,
In his large tolerant wisdom,
Filled with the ardours of earth
Her twenty summers?

Well did he make her for loving;
Well did he mould her for beauty;
Gave her the wish that is brave
With understanding.

"O Pan, avert from this maiden
Sorrow, misfortune, bereavement,
Harm, and unhappy regret,"
Prays one fond mortal.

XLV - Softer Than the Hill Fog to the Forest

Softer than the hill-fog to the forest
Are the loving hands of my dear lover,
When she sleeps beside me in the starlight
And her beauty drenches me with rest.

As the quiet mist enfolds the beech-trees,
Even as she dreams her arms enfold me,
Half awaking with a hundred kisses
On the scarlet lily of her mouth.

XLVI - I Seek and Desire

I seek and desire,
Even as the wind
That travels the plain
And stirs in the bloom
Of the apple-tree.

I wander through life,
With the searching mind
That is never at rest,
Till I reach the shade
Of my lover's door.

XLVII - Like Torn Sea Kelp in the Drift

Like torn sea-kelp in the drift
Of the great tides of the sea,
Carried past the harbour-mouth

To the deep beyond return,

I am buoyed and borne away
On the loveliness of earth,
Little caring, save for thee,
Past the portals of the night.

XLVIII - Fine Woven Purple Linen

Fine woven purple linen
I bring thee from Phocaea,
That, beauty upon beauty,
A precious gift may cover
The lap where I have lain.

And a gold comb, and girdle,
And trinkets of white silver,
And gems are in my sea-chest,
Lest poor and empty-handed
Thy lover should return.

And I have brought from Tyre
A Pan-flute stained vermilion,
Wherein the gods have hidden
Love and desire and longing,
Which I shall loose for thee.

XLIX - When I Am Home From Travel

When I am home from travel,
My eager foot will stay not
Until I reach the threshold
Where I went forth from thee.

And there, as darkness gathers
In the rose-scented garden,
The god who prospers music
Shall give me skill to play.

And thou shalt hear, all startled,
A flute blown in the twilight,
With the soft pleading magic
The green wood heard of old.

Then, lamp in hand, thy beauty
In the rose-marble entry!
And unreluctant Hermes
Shall give me words to say.

L - When I Behold the Pharos Shine

When I behold the pharos shine
And lay a path along the sea,
How gladly I shall feel the spray,
Standing upon the swinging prow;

And question of my pilot old,
How many watery leagues to sail
Ere we shall round the harbour reef
And anchor off the wharves of home!

LI - Is the Day Long

Is the day long,
O Lesbian maiden,
And the night endless
In thy lone chamber
In Mitylene?

All the bright day,
Until welcome evening
When the stars kindle
Over the harbour,
What tasks employ thee?

Passing the fountain
At golden sundown,
One of the home-going
Traffickers, hast thou
Thought of thy lover?

Nay, but how far
Too brief will the night be,
When I returning
To the dear portal
Hear my own heart beat!

LII - Lo, On the Distance a Dark Blue Ravine

Lo, on the distance a dark blue ravine,
A fold in the mountainous forests of fir,
Cleft from the sky-line sheer down to the shore!

Above are the clouds and the white, pealing gulls,
At its foot is the rough broken foam of the sea,
With ever anon the long deep muffled roar,—
A sigh from the fitful great heart of the world.

Then inland just where the small meadow begins,
Well bulwarked with boulders that jut in the tide,
Lies safe beyond storm-beat the harbour in sun.

See where the black fishing-boats, each at its buoy,
Ride up on the swell with their dare-danger prows,
To sight o'er the sea-rim what venture may come!

And look, where the narrow white streets of the town
Leap up from the blue water's edge to the wood,
Scant room for man's range between mountain and sea,
And the market where woodsmen from over the hill
May traffic, and sailors from far foreign ports
With treasure brought in from the ends of the earth.

And see the third house on the left, with that gleam
Of red burnished copper—the hinge of the door
Whereat I shall enter, expected so oft
(Let love be your sea-star!), to voyage no more.

LIII - Art Thou the Topmost Apple

Art thou the top-most apple
The gatherers could not reach,
Reddening on the bough?
Shall not I take thee?

Art thou a hyacinth blossom
The shepherds upon the hills
Have trodden into the ground?
Shall not I lift thee?

Free is the young god Eros,
Paying no tribute to power,

Seeing no evil in beauty,
Full of compassion.

Once having found the beloved,
However sorry or woeful,
However scornful of loving,
Little it matters.

LIV - How Soon Will All My Lovely Days Be Over

How soon will all my lovely days be over,
And I no more be found beneath the sun,—
Neither beside the many-murmuring sea,
Nor where the plain-winds whisper to the reeds,
Nor in the tall beech-woods among the hills
Where roam the bright-lipped Oreads, nor along
The pasture-sides where berry-pickers stray
And harmless shepherds pipe their sheep to fold!

For I am eager, and the flame of life
Burns quickly in the fragile lamp of clay.
Passion and love and longing and hot tears
Consume this mortal Sappho, and too soon
A great wind from the dark will blow upon me,
And I be no more found in the fair world,
For all the search of the revolving moon
And patient shine of everlasting stars.

LV - Soul of Sorrow, Why This Weeping?

Soul of sorrow, why this weeping?
What immortal grief hath touched thee
With the poignancy of sadness,—
Testament of tears?

Have the high gods deigned to show thee
Destiny, and disillusion
Fills thy heart at all things human,
Fleeting and desired?

Nay, the gods themselves are fettered
By one law which links together
Truth and nobleness and beauty,
Man and stars and sea.

And they only shall find freedom
Who with courage rise and follow
Where love leads beyond all peril,
Wise beyond all words.

LVI - It Never Can Be Mine

It never can be mine
To sit in the door in the sun
And watch the world go by,
A pageant and a dream;

For I was born for love,
And fashioned for desire,
Beauty, passion, and joy,
And sorrow and unrest;

And with all things of earth
Eternally must go,
Daring the perilous bourn
Of joyance and of death,

A strain of song by night,
A shadow on the hill,
A hint of odorous grass,
A murmur of the sea.

LVII - Others Shall Behold the Sun

Others shall behold the sun
Through the long uncounted years,—
Not a maid in after time
Wise as thou!

For the gods have given thee
Their best gift, an equal mind
That can only love, be glad,
And fear not.

LVIII - Let Thy Strong Spirit Never Fear

Let thy strong spirit never fear,

Nor in thy virgin soul be thou afraid.
The gods themselves and the almightier fates
Cannot avail to harm

With outward and misfortunate chance
The radiant unshaken mind of him
Who at his being's centre will abide,
Secure from doubt and fear.

His wise and patient heart shall share
The strong sweet loveliness of all things made,
And the serenity of inward joy
Beyond the storm of tears.

LIX - Will None Say of Sappho

Will none say of Sappho,
Speaking of her lovers,
And the love they gave her, —
Joy and days and beauty,
Flute-playing and roses,
Song and wine and laughter, —

Will none, musing, murmur,
"Yet, for all the roses,
All the flutes and lovers,
Doubt not she was lonely
As the sea, whose cadence
Haunts the world for ever."

LX - When I Have Departed

When I have departed,
Say but this behind me,
"Love was all her wisdom,
All her care.

"Well she kept love's secret, —
Dared and never faltered, —
Laughed and never doubted
Love would win.

"Let the world's rough triumph
Trample by above her,

She is safe forever
From all harm.

"In a land that knows not
Bitterness nor sorrow,
She has found out all
Of truth at last."

LXI - There is No More to Say, Now Thou Art Still

There is no more to say now thou art still,
There is no more to do now thou art dead,
There is no more to know now thy clear mind
Is back returned unto the gods who gave it.

Now thou art gone the use of life is past,
The meaning and the glory and the pride,
There is no joyous friend to share the day,
And on the threshold no awaited shadow.

LXII - Play Up, Play Up Thy Silver Flute

Play up, play up thy silver flute;
The crickets all are brave;
Glad is the red autumnal earth
And the blue sea.

Play up thy flawless silver flute;
Dead ripe are fruit and grain.
When love puts on his scarlet coat,
Put off thy care.

LXIII - A Beautiful Child is Mine

A beautiful child is mine,
Formed like a golden flower,
Cleis the loved one.
And above her I value
Not all the Lydian land,
Nor lovely Hellas.

LXIV - Ah, But Now Henceforth

Ah, but now henceforth
Only one meaning
Has life for me.

Only one purport,
Measure and beauty,
Has the bright world.

What mean the wood-winds,
Colour and morning,
Bird, stream, and hill?

And the brave city
With its enchantment?
Thee, only thee!

LXV - Softly the Wind Moves Through the Radiant Morning

Softly the wind moves through the radiant morning,
And the warm sunlight sinks into the valley,
Filling the green earth with a quiet joyance,
Strength, and fulfilment.

Even so, gentle, strong and wise and happy,
Through the soul and substance of my being,
Comes the breath of thy great love to me-ward,
O thou dear mortal.

LXVI - What the West Wind Whispers

What the west wind whispers
At the end of summer,
When the barley harvest
Ripens to the sickle,
Who can tell?

What means the fine music
Of the dry cicada,
Through the long noon hours
Of the autumn stillness,
Who can say?

How the grape ungathered
With its bloom of blueness
Greatens on the trellis
Of the brick-walled garden,
Who can know?

Yet I, too, am greatened,
Keep the note of gladness,
Travel by the wind's road,
Through this autumn leisure,—
By thy love.

LXVII - Indoors the Fire is Kindled

Indoors the fire is kindled;
Beechwood is piled on the hearthstone;
Cold are the chattering oak-leaves;
And the ponds frost-bitten.

Softer than rainfall at twilight,
Bringing the fields benediction
And the hills quiet and greyness,
Are my long thoughts of thee.

How should thy friend fear the seasons?
They only perish of winter
Whom Love, audacious and tender,
Never hath visited.

LXVIII - You Ask How Love Can Keep the Mortal Soul

You ask how love can keep the mortal soul
Strong to the pitch of joy throughout the years.

Ask how your brave cicada on the bough
Keeps the long sweet insistence of his cry;

Ask how the Pleiads steer across the night
In their serene unswerving mighty course;

Ask how the wood-flowers waken to the sun,
Unsummoned save by some mysterious word;

Ask how the wandering swallows find your eaves
Upon the rain-wind with returning spring;

Ask who commands the ever-punctual tide
To keep the pendulous rhythm of the sea;

And you shall know what leads the heart of man
To the far haven of his hopes and fears.

LXIX - Like a Tall Forest Were Their Spears

Like a tall forest were their spears,
Their banners like a silken sea,
When the great host in splendour passed
Across the crimson sinking sun.

And then the bray of brazen horns
Arose above their clanking march,
As the long waving column filed
Into the odorous purple dusk.

O lover, in this radiant world
Whence is the race of mortal men,
So frail, so mighty, and so fond,
That fleets into the vast unknown?

LXX - My Lover Smiled, "O Friend, Ask Not

My lover smiled, "O friend, ask not
The journey's end, nor whence we are.
That whistling boy who minds his goats
So idly in the grey ravine,

"The brown-backed rower drenched with spray,
The lemon-seller in the street,
And the young girl who keeps her first
Wild love-tryst at the rising moon,—

"Lo, these are wiser than the wise.
And not for all our questioning
Shall we discover more than joy,
Nor find a better thing than love!

"Let pass the banners and the spears,

The hate, the battle, and the greed;
For greater than all gifts is peace,
And strength is in the tranquil mind."

LXXI - Ye Who Have the Stable World

Ye who have the stable world
In the keeping of your hands.
Flocks and men, the lasting hills,
And the ever-wheeling stars;

Ye who freight with wondrous things
The wide-wandering heart of man
And the galleon of the moon,
On those silent seas of foam;

Oh, if ever ye shall grant
Time and place and room enough
To this fond and fragile heart
Stifled with the throb of love,

On that day one grave-eyed Fate,
Pausing in her toil, shall say,
"Lo, one mortal has achieved
Immortality of love!"

LXXII - I Heard the Gods Reply

I heard the gods reply:
"Trust not the future with its perilous chance;
The fortunate hour is on the dial now.

"To-day be wise and great,
And put off hesitation and go forth
With cheerful courage for the diurnal need.

"Stout be the heart, nor slow
The foot to follow the impetuous will,
Nor the hand slack upon the loom of deeds.

"Then may the Fates look up
And smile a little in their tolerant way,
Being full of infinite regard for men."

LXXIII - The Sun On the Tide, the Peach On the Bough

The sun on the tide, the peach on the bough,
The blue smoke over the hill,
And the shadows trailing the valley-side,
Make up the autumn day.

Ah, no, not half! Thou art not here
Under the bronze beech-leaves,
And thy lover's soul like a lonely child
Roams through an empty room.

LXXIV - If Death Be Good

If death be good,
Why do the gods not die?
If life be ill,
Why do the gods still live?

If love be naught,
Why do the gods still love?
If love be all,
What should men do but love?

LXXV - Tell Me What This Life Means

Tell me what this life means,
O my prince and lover,
With the autumn sunlight
On thy bronze-gold head?

With thy clear voice sounding
Through the silver twilight,—
What is the lost secret
Of the tacit earth?

LXXVI - Ye Have Heard How Marsyas

Ye have heard how Marsyas,
In the folly of his pride,

Boasted of a matchless skill,—
When the great god's back was turned;

How his fond imagining
Fell to ashes cold and grey,
When the flawless player came
In serenity and light.

So it was with those I loved
In the years ere I loved thee.
Many a saying sounds like truth,
Until Truth itself is heard.

Many a beauty only lives
Until Beauty passes by,
And the mortal is forgot
In the shadow of the god.

LXXVII - Hour By Hour I Sit

Hour by hour I sit,
Watching the silent door.
Shadows go by on the wall,
And steps in the street.

Expectation and doubt
Flutter my timorous heart.
So many hurrying home—
And thou still away.

LXXVIII - Once in the Shining Street

Once in the shining street,
In the heart of a seaboard town,
As I waited, behold, there came
The woman I loved.

As when, in the early spring,
A daffodil blooms in the grass,
Golden and gracious and glad,
The solitude smiled.

LXXIX - How Strange is Love, O My Lover

How strange is love, O my lover!
With what enchantment and power
Does it not come upon mortals,
Learned or heedless!

How far away and unreal,
Faint as blue isles in a sunset
Haze-golden, all else of life seems,
Since I have known thee!

LXXX - How to Say I Love You

How to say I love you:
What, if I but live it,
Were the use in that, love?
Small, indeed.

Only, every moment
Of this waking lifetime
Let me be your lover
And your friend!

Ah, but then, as sure as
Blossom breaks from bud-sheath,
When along the hillside
Spring returns,

Golden speech should flower
From the soul so cherished,
And the mouth your kisses
Filled with fire.

LXXXI - Hark, Love, to the Tambourines

Hark, love, to the tambourines
Of the minstrels in the street,
And one voice that throbs and soars
Clear above the clashing time!

Some Egyptian royal love-lilt,
Some Sidonian refrain,
Vows of Paphos or of Tyre,

Mount against the silver sun.

Pleading, piercing, yet serene,
Vagrant in a foreign town,
From what passion was it born,
In what lost land over sea?

LXXXII - Over the Roofs the Honey Coloured Moon

Over the roofs the honey-coloured moon,
With purple shadows on the silver grass,

And the warm south-wind on the curving sea,
While we two, lovers past all turmoil now,

Watch from the window the white sails come in,
Bearing what unknown ventures safe to port!

So falls the hour of twilight and of love
With wizardry to loose the hearts of men,

And there is nothing more in this great world
Than thou and I, and the blue dome of dusk.

LXXXIII - In the Quiet Garden World

In the quiet garden world,
Gold sunlight and shadow leaves
Flicker on the wall.

And the wind, a moment since,
With rose-petals strewed the path
And the open door.

Now the moon-white butterflies
Float across the liquid air,
Glad as in a dream;

And, across thy lover's heart,
Visions of one scarlet mouth
With its maddening smile.

LXXXIV - Soft Was the Wind in the Beech Trees

Soft was the wind in the beech-trees;
Low was the surf on the shore;
In the blue dusk one planet
Like a great sea-pharos shone.

But nothing to me were the sea-sounds,
The wind and the yellow star,
When over my breast the banner
Of your golden hair was spread.

LXXXV - Have Ye Heard the News of Sappho's Garden

Have you heard the news of Sappho's garden,
And the Golden Rose of Mitylene,
Which the bending brown-armed rowers lately
Brought from over sea, from lonely Pontus?

In a meadow by the river Halys,
Where some wood-god hath the world in keeping,
On a burning summer noon they found her,
Lovely as a Dryad, and more tender.

Her these eyes have seen, and not another
Shall behold, till time takes all things goodly,
So surpassing fair and fond and wondrous,—
Such a slave as, worth a great king's ransom,

No man yet of all the sons of mortals
But would lose his soul for and regret not;
So hath Beauty compassed all her children
With the cords of longing and desire.

Only Hermes, master of word music,
Ever yet in glory of gold language
Could ensphere the magical remembrance
Of her melting, half sad, wayward beauty,

Or devise the silver phrase to frame her,
The inevitable name to call her,
Half a sigh and half a kiss when whispered,
Like pure air that feeds a forge's hunger.

Not a painter in the Isles of Hellas
Could portray her, mix the golden tawny

With bright stain of poppies, or ensanguine
Like the life her darling mouth's vermilion,

So that, in the ages long hereafter,
When we shall be dust of perished summers,
Any man could say who found that likeness,
Smiling gently on it, "This was Gorgo!"

LXXXVI - Love is So Strong a Thing

Love is so strong a thing,
The very gods must yield,
When it is welded fast
With the unflinching truth.

Love is so frail a thing,
A word, a look, will kill.
Oh lovers, have a care
How ye do deal with love.

LXXXVII - Hadst Thou with All Thy Loveliness Been True

Hadst thou, with all thy loveliness, been true,
Had I, with all my tenderness, been strong,
We had not made this ruin out of life,
This desolation in a world of joy,
My poor Gorgo.

Yet even the high gods at times do err;
Be therefore thou not overcome with woe,
But dedicate anew to greater love
An equal heart, and be thy radiant self
Once more, Gorgo.

LXXXVIII - As On a Morn a Traveller Might Emerge

As, on a morn, a traveller might emerge
From the deep green seclusion of the hills,
By a cool road through forest and through fern,
Little frequented, winding, followed long
With joyous expectation and day-dreams,
And on a sudden, turning a great rock

Covered with frondage, dark with dripping water,
Behold the seaboard full of surf and sound,
With all the space and glory of the world
Above the burnished silver of the sea,—

Even so it was upon that first spring day
When time, that is a devious path for men,
Led me all lonely to thy door at last;
And all thy splendid beauty, gracious and glad,
(Glad as bright colour, free as wind or air,
And lovelier than racing seas of foam)
Bore sense and soul and mind at once away
To a pure region where the gods might dwell,
Making of me, a vagrant child before,
A servant of joy at Aphrodite's will.

LXXXIX - Where Shall I Look For Thee

Where shall I look for thee,
Where find thee now,
O my lost Atthis?

Storm bars the harbour,
And snow keeps the pass
In the blue mountains.

Bitter the wind whistles,
Pale is the sun,
And the days shorten.

Close to the hearthstone,
With long thoughts of thee,
Thy lonely lover

Sits now, remembering
All the spent hours
And thy fair beauty.

Ah, when the hyacinth
Wakens with spring,
And buds the laurel,

Doubt not, some morning
When all earth revives,
Hearing Pan's flute-call

Over the river-beds,
Over the hills,
Sounding the summons,

I shall look up and behold
In the door,
Smiling, expectant,

Loving as ever
And glad as of old,
My own lost Atthis!

XC - O Sad, Sad Face and Saddest Eyes That Ever

A sad, sad face, and saddest eyes that ever
Beheld the sun,
Whence came the grief that makes of all thy beauty
One sad sweet smile?

In this bright portrait, where the painter fixed them,
I still behold
The eyes that gladdened, and the lips that loved me,
And, gold on rose,

The cloud of hair that settles on one shoulder
Slipped from its vest.
I almost hear thy Mitylenean love-song
In the spring night,

When the still air was odorous with blossoms,
And in the hour
Thy first wild girl's-love trembled into being,
Glad, glad and fond.

Ah, where is all that wonder? What god's malice
Undid that joy
And set the seal of patient woe upon thee,
O my lost love?

XCI - Why Have the Gods in Derision

Why have the gods in derision
Severed us, heart of my being?
Where have they lured thee to wander,

O my lost lover?

While now I sojourn with sorrow,
Having remorse for my comrade,
What town is blessed with thy beauty,
Gladdened and prospered?

Nay, who could love as I loved thee,
With whom thy beauty was mingled
In those spring days when the swallows
Came with the south wind?

Then I became as that shepherd
Loved by Selene on Latmus,
Once when her own summer magic
Took hold upon her

With a sweet madness, and thenceforth
Her mortal lover must wander
Over the wide world for ever,
Like one enchanted.

XCII - Like a Red Lily in the Meadow Grasses

Like a red lily in the meadow grasses,
Swayed by the wind and burning in the sunlight,
I saw you, where the city chokes with traffic,
Bearing among the passers-by your beauty,
Unsullied, wild, and delicate as a flower.
And then I knew, past doubt or peradventure,
Our loved and mighty Eleusinian mother
Had taken thought of me for her pure worship,
And of her favour had assigned my comrade
For the Great Mysteries,—knew I should find you
When the dusk murmured with its new-made lovers,
And we be no more foolish but wise children,
And well content partake of joy together,
As she ordains and human hearts desire.

XCIII - When in the Spring the Swallows All Return

When in the spring the swallows all return,
And the bleak bitter sea grows mild once more,
With all its thunders softened to a sigh;

When to the meadows the young green comes back,
And swelling buds put forth on every bough,
With wild-wood odours on the delicate air;

Ah, then, in that so lovely earth wilt thou
With all thy beauty love me all one way,
And make me all thy lover as before?

Lo, where the white-maned horses of the surge,
Plunging in thunderous onset to the shore,
Trample and break and charge along the sand!

XCIV - Cold is the Wind Where Daphne Sleeps

Cold is the wind where Daphne sleeps,
That was so tender and so warm
With loving,—with a loveliness
Than her own laurel lovelier.

Now pipes the bitter wind for her,
And the snow sifts about her door,
While far below her frosty hill
The racing billows plunge and boom.

XCV - Hark, Where Poseidon's

Hark, where Poseidon's
White racing horses
Trample with tumult
The shelving seaboard!

Older than Saturn,
Older than Rhea,
That mournful music,
Falling and surging

With the vast rhythm
Ceaseless, eternal,
Keeps the long tally
Of all things mortal.

How many lovers
Hath not its lulling

Cradled to slumber
With the ripe flowers,

Ere for our pleasure
This golden summer
Walked through the corn-lands
In gracious splendour!

How many loved ones
Will it not croon to,
In the long spring-days
Through coming ages,

When all our day-dreams
Have been forgotten,
And none remembers
Even thy beauty!

They too shall slumber
In quiet places,
And mighty sea-sounds
Call them unheeded.

XCVI - Hark, My Lover, it is Spring!

Hark, my lover, it is spring!
On the wind a faint far call
Wakes a pang within my heart,
Unmistakable and keen.

At the harbour mouth a sail
Glimmers in the morning sun,
And the ripples at her prow
Whiten into crumbling foam,

As she forges outward bound
For the teeming foreign ports.
Through the open window now,
Hear the sailors lift a song!

In the meadow ground the frogs
With their deafening flutes begin,—
The old madness of the world
In their golden throats again.

Little fifers of live bronze,

Who hath taught you with wise lore
To unloose the strains of joy,
When Orion seeks the west?

And you feathered flute-players,
Who instructed you to fill
All the blossomy orchards now
With melodious desire?

I doubt not our father Pan
Hath a care of all these things.
In some valley of the hills
Far away and misty-blue,

By quick water he hath cut
A new pipe, and set the wood
To his smiling lips, and blown,
That earth's rapture be restored.

And those wild Pandean stops
Mark the cadence life must keep.
O my lover, be thou glad;
It is spring in Hellas now.

XCVII - When the Early Soft Spring Wind Comes Blowing

When the early soft spring wind comes blowing
Over Rhodes and Samos and Miletus,
From the seven mouths of Nile to Lesbos,
Freighted with sea-odours and gold sunshine,

What news spreads among the island people
In the market-place of Mitylene,
Lending that unwonted stir of gladness
To the busy streets and thronging doorways?

Is it word from Ninus or Arbela,
Babylon the great, or Northern Imbros?
Have the laden galleons been sighted
Stoutly labouring up the sea from Tyre?

Nay, 'tis older news that foreign sailor
With the cheek of sea-tan stops to prattle
To the young fig-seller with her basket
And the breasts that bud beneath her tunic,

And I hear it in the rustling tree-tops.
All this passionate bright tender body
Quivers like a leaf the wind has shaken,
Now love wanders through the aisles of springtime.

XCVIII - I Am More Tremulous Than Shaken Reeds

I am more tremulous than shaken reeds,
And love has made me like the river water.

Thy voice is as the hill-wind over me,
And all my changing heart gives heed, my lover.

Before thy least lost murmur I must sigh,
Or gladden with thee as the sun-path glitters.

XCIX - Over the Wheat Field

Over the wheat-field,
Over the hill-crest,
Swoops and is gone
The beat of a wild wing,
Brushing the pine-tops,
Bending the poppies,
Hurrying Northward
With golden summer.

What premonition,
O purple swallow,
Told thee the happy
Hour of migration?
Hark! On the threshold
(Hush, flurried heart in me!),
Was there a footfall?
Did no one enter?

Soon will a shepherd
In rugged Dacia,
Folding his gentle
Ewes in the twilight,
Lifting a level
Gaze from the sheepfold,
Say to his fellows,
"Lo, it is springtime."

This very hour
In Mitylene,
Will not a young girl
Say to her lover,
Lifting her moon-white
Arms to enlace him,
Ere the glad sigh comes,
"Lo, it is lovetime!"

C - Once More the Rain on the Mountain

Once more the rain on the mountain,
Once more the wind in the valley,
With the soft odours of springtime
And the long breath of remembrance,
O Lityerses!

Warm is the sun in the city.
On the street corners with laughter
Traffic the flower-girls. Beauty
Blossoms once more for thy pleasure
In many places.

Gentlier now falls the twilight,
With the slim moon in the pear-trees;
And the green frogs in the meadows
Blow on shrill pipes to awaken
Thee, Lityerses.

Gladlier now crimson morning
Flushes fair-built Mitylene,—
Portico, temple, and column,—
Where the young garlanded women
Praise thee with singing.

Ah, but what burden of sorrow
Tinges their slow stately chorus,
Though spring revisits the glad earth?
Wilt thou not wake to their summons,
O Lityerses?

Shall they then never behold thee,—
Nevermore see thee returning
Down the blue cleft of the mountains,
Nor in the purple of evening

Welcome thy coming?

Nevermore answer thy glowing
Youth with their ardour, nor cherish
With lovely longing thy spirit,
Nor with soft laughter beguile thee,
O Lityerses?

Heedless, assuaged, art thou sleeping
Where the spring sun cannot find thee,
Nor the wind waken, nor woodlands
Bloom for thy innocent rapture
Through golden hours?

Hast thou no passion nor pity
For thy deserted companions?
Never again will thy beauty
Quell their desire nor rekindle,
O Lityerses?

Nay, but in vain their clear voices
Call thee. Thy sensitive beauty
Is become part of the fleeting
Loveliness, merged in the pathos
Of all things mortal.

In the faint fragrance of flowers,
On the sweet draft of the sea-wind,
Linger strange hints now that loosen
Tears for thy gay gentle spirit,
O Lityerses!

Epilogue

Now the hundred songs are made,
And the pause comes. Loving Heart,
There must be an end to summer,
And the flute be laid aside.

On a day the frost will come,
Walking through the autumn world,
Hushing all the brave endeavour
Of the crickets in the grass.

On a day (Oh, far from now!)
Earth will hear this voice no more;

For it shall be with thy lover
As with Linus long ago.

All the happy songs he wrought
From remembrance soon must fade,
As the wash of silver moonlight
From a purple-dark ravine.

Frail as dew upon the grass
Or the spindrift of the sea,
Out of nothing they were fashioned
And to nothing must return.

Nay, but something of thy love,
Passion, tenderness, and joy,
Some strange magic of thy beauty,
Some sweet pathos of thy tears,

Must imperishably cling
To the cadence of the words,
Like a spell of lost enchantments
Laid upon the hearts of men.

Wild and fleeting as the notes
Blown upon a woodland pipe,
They must haunt the earth with gladness
And a tinge of old regret.

For the transport in their rhythm
Was the throb of thy desire,
And thy lyric moods shall quicken
Souls of lovers yet unborn.

When the golden days arrive,
With the swallow at the eaves,
And the first sob of the south-wind
Sighing at the latch with spring,

Long hereafter shall thy name
Be recalled through foreign lands,
And thou be a part of sorrow
When the Linus songs are sung.

Bliss Carman - An Appreciation

How many Canadians—how many even among the few who seek to keep themselves informed of the best in contemporary literature, who are ever on the alert for the new voices—realise, or even suspect, that this Northern land of theirs has produced a poet of whom it may be affirmed with confidence and assurance that he is of the great succession of English poets? Yet such—strange and unbelievable though it may seem—is in very truth the case, that poet being (to give him his full name) William Bliss Carman. Canada has full right to be proud of her poets, a small body though they are; but not only does Mr. Carman stand high and clear above them all—his place (and time cannot but confirm and justify the assertion) is among those men whose poetry is the shining glory of that great English literature which is our common heritage.

If any should ask why, if what has been just said is so, there has been—as must be admitted—no general recognition of the fact in the poet's home land, I would answer that there are various and plausible, if not good, reasons for it.

First of all, the poet, as thousands more of our young men of ambition and confidence have done, went early to the United States, and until recently, except for rare and brief visits to his old home down by the sea, has never returned to Canada—though for all that, I am able to state, on his own authority, he is still a Canadian citizen. Then all his books have had their original publication in the United States, and while a few of them have subsequently carried the imprints of Canadian publishers, none of these can be said ever to have made any special effort to push their sale. Another reason for the fact above mentioned is that Mr. Carman has always scorned to advertise himself, while his work has never been the subject of the log-rolling and booming which the work of many another poet has had—to his ultimate loss. A further reason is that he follows a rule of his own in preparing his books for publication. Most poets publish a volume of their work as soon as, through their industry and perseverance, they have material enough on hand to make publication desirable in their eyes. Not so with Mr. Carman, however, his rule being not to publish until he has done sufficient work of a certain general character or key to make a volume. As a result, you cannot fully know or estimate his work by one book, or two books, or even half a dozen; you must possess or be familiar with every one of the score and more volumes which contain his output of poetry before you can realise how great and how many-sided is his genius.

It is a common remark on the part of those who respond readily to the vigorous work of Kipling, or Masefield, even our own Service, that Bliss Carman's poetry has no relation to or concern with ordinary, everyday life. One would suppose that most persons who cared for poetry at all turned to it as a relief from or counter to the burdens and vexations of the daily round; but in any event, the remark referred to seems to me to indicate either the most casual acquaintance with Mr. Carman's work, or a complete misunderstanding and misapprehension of the meaning of it. I grant that you will find little or nothing in it all to remind you of the grim realities and vexing social problems of this modern existence of ours; but to say or to suggest that these things do not exist for Mr. Carman is to say or to suggest something which is the reverse of true. The truth is, he is aware of them as only one with the sensitive organism of a poet can be; but he does not feel that he has a call or mission to remedy them, and still less to sing of them. He therefore leaves the immediate problems of the day to those who choose, or are led, to occupy themselves therewith, and turns resolutely away to dwell upon those things which for him possess infinitely greater importance.

"What are they?" one who knows Mr. Carman only as, say, a lyrist of spring or as a singer of the delights of vagabondia probably will ask in some wonder. Well, the things which concern him above all, I would answer, are first, and naturally, the beauty and wonder of this world of ours, and next the mystery of the earthly pilgrimage of the human soul out of eternity and back into it again.

The poems in the present volume—which, by the way, can boast the high honor of being the very first regular Canadian edition of his work—will be evidence ample and conclusive to every reader, I am sure, of the place which

The perennial enchanted
Lovely world and all its lore

occupy in the heart and soul of Bliss Carman, as well as of the magical power with which he is able to convey the deep and unfailing satisfaction and delight which they possess for him. They, however, represent his latest period (he has had three well-defined periods), comprising selections from three of his last published volumes: The Rough Rider, Echoes from Vagabondia, and April Airs, together with a number of new poems, and do not show, except here and there and by hints and flashes, how great is his preoccupation with the problem of man's existence—

—the hidden import
Of man's eternal plight.

This is manifest most in certain of his earlier books, for in these he turns and returns to the greatest of all the problems of man almost constantly, probing, with consummate and almost unrivalled use of the art of expression, for the secret which surely, he clearly feels, lies hidden somewhere, to be discovered if one could but pierce deeply enough. Pick up Behind the Arras, and as you turn over page after page you cannot but observe how incessantly the poet's mind—like the minds of his two great masters, Browning and Whitman—works at this problem. In "Behind the Arras," the title poem; "In the Wings," "The Crimson House," "The Lodger," "Beyond the Gamut," "The Juggler"—yes, in every poem in the book—he takes up and handles the strange thing we know as, or call, life, turning it now this way, now that, in an effort to find out its meaning and purpose. He comes but little nearer success in this than do most of the rest of men, of course; but the magical and ever-fresh beauty of his expression, the haunting melody of his lines, the variety of his images and figures and the depth and range of his thought, put his searchings and ponderings in a class by themselves.

Lengthy quotation from Mr. Carman's books is not permitted here, and I must guide myself accordingly, though with reluctance, because I believe that in a study such as this the subject should be allowed to speak for himself as much as possible. In "Behind the Arras" the poet describes the passage from life to death as

A cadence dying down unto its source
In music's course,

and goes on to speak of death as

—the broken rhythm of thought and man,
The sweep and span
Of memory and hope
About the orbit where they still must grope
For wider scope,

To be through thousand springs restored, renewed,
With love imbrued,

With increments of will
Made strong, perceiving unattainment still
From each new skill.

Now follow some verses from "Behind the Gamut," to my mind the poet's greatest single achievement;

As fine sand spread on a disc of silver,
At some chord which bids the motes combine,
Heeding the hidden and reverberant impulse,
Shifts and dances into curve and line,

The round earth, too, haply, like a dust-mote,
Was set whirling her assigned sure way,
Round this little orb of her ecliptic
To some harmony she must obey.

And what of man?

Linked to all his half-accomplished fellows,
Through unfrontiered provinces to range—
Man is but the morning dream of nature,
Roused to some wild cadence weird and strange.

Here, now, are some verses from "Pulvis et Umbra," which is to be found in Mr. Carman's first book, Low Tide on Grand Pré, and in which the poet addresses a moth which a storm has blown into his window:

For man walks the world with mourning
Down to death and leaves no trace,
With the dust upon his forehead,
And the shadow on his face.

Pillared dust and fleeing shadow
As the roadside wind goes by,
And the fourscore years that vanish
In the twinkling of an eye.

"Pillared dust and fleeing shadow." Where in all our English literature will one find the life history of man summed up more briefly and, at the same time, more beautifully, than in that wonderful line? Now follows a companion verse to those just quoted, taken from "Lord of My Heart's Elation," which stands in the forefront of From the Green Book of the Bards. It may be remarked here that while the poet recurs again and again to some favorite thought or idea, it is never in the same words. His expression is always new and fresh, showing how deep and true is his inspiration. Again it is man who is pictured:

A fleet and shadowy column
Of dust and mountain rain,
To walk the earth a moment
And be dissolved again.

But while Mr. Carman's speculations upon life's meaning and the mystery of the future cannot but appeal to the thoughtful-minded, it is as an interpreter of nature that he makes his widest appeal. Bliss Carman, I must say here, and emphatically, is no mere landscape-painter; he never, or scarcely ever, paints a picture of nature for its own sake. He goes beyond the outward aspect of things and interprets or translates for us with less keen senses as only a poet whose feeling for nature is of the deepest and profoundest, who has gone to her whole-heartedly and been taken close to her warm bosom, can do. Is this not evident from these verses from "The Great Return"—originally called "The Pagan's Prayer," and for some inscrutable reason to be found only in the limited Collected Poems, issued in two stately volumes in 1905.

When I have lifted up my heart to thee,
Thou hast ever hearkened and drawn near,
And bowed thy shining face close over me,
Till I could hear thee as the hill-flowers hear.

When I have cried to thee in lonely need,
Being but a child of thine bereft and wrung,
Then all the rivers in the hills gave heed;
And the great hill-winds in thy holy tongue—

That ancient incommunicable speech—
The April stars and autumn sunsets know—
Soothed me and calmed with solace beyond reach
Of human ken, mysterious and low.

Who can read or listen to those moving lines without feeling that Mr. Carman is in very truth a poet of nature—nay, Nature's own poet? But how could he be other when, in "The Breath of the Reed" (From the Green Book of the Bards), he makes the appeal?

Make me thy priest, O Mother,
And prophet of thy mood,
With all the forest wonder
Enraptured and imbued.

As becomes such a poet, and particularly a poet whose birth-month is April, Mr. Carman sings much of the early spring. Again and again he takes up his woodland pipe, and lo! Pan himself and all his train troop joyously before us. Yet the singer's notes for all his singing never become wearied or strident; his airs are ever new and fresh; his latest songs are no less spontaneous and winning than were his first, written how many years ago, while at the same time they have gained in beauty and melody. What heart will not stir to the vibrant music of his immortal "Spring Song," which was originally published in the first Songs from Vagabondia, and the opening verses of which follow?

Make me over, mother April,
When the sap begins to stir!
When thy flowery hand delivers
All the mountain-prisoned rivers,
And thy great heart beats and quivers
To revive the days that were,

Make me over, mother April,
When the sap begins to stir!

Take my dust and all my dreaming,
Count my heart-beats one by one,
Send them where the winters perish;
Then some golden noon recherish
And restore them in the sun,
Flower and scent and dust and dreaming,
With their heart-beats every one!

That poem is sufficient in itself to prove that Bliss Carman has full right and title to be called Spring's own lyrist, though it may be remarked here that not all his spring poems are so unfeignedly joyous. Many of them indeed, have a touch, or more than a touch, of wistfulness, for the poet knows well that sorrow lurks under all joy, deep and well hidden though it may be.

Mr. Carman sings equally finely, though perhaps not so frequently, of summer and the other seasons; but as he has other claims upon our attention, I shall forbear to labor the fact, particularly as the following collection demonstrates it sufficiently. One of those other claims is as a writer of sea poetry. Few poets, it may be said, have pictured the majesty and the mystery, the beauty and the terror of the sea, better than he. His Ballads of Lost Haven is a veritable treasure-house for those whose spirits find kinship in wide expanses of moving waters. One of the best known poems in this volume is "The Gravedigger," which opens thus:

Oh, the shambling sea is a sexton old,
And well his work is done.
With an equal grave for lord and knave,
He buries them every one.

Then hoy and rip, with a rolling hip,
He makes for the nearest shore;
And God, who sent him a thousand ship,
Will send him a thousand more;
But some he'll save for a bleaching grave,
And shoulder them in to shore—
Shoulder them in, shoulder them in,
Shoulder them in to shore.

In "The City of the Sea" (Last Songs from Vagabondia) Mr. Carman speaks of the seabells sounding

The eternal cadence of sea sorrow
For Man's lot and immemorial wrong—
The lost strains that haunt the human dwelling
With the ghost of song.

Elsewhere he speaks of

The great sea, mystic and musical.

And here from another poem is a striking picture:

... the old sea
Seems to whimper and deplore
Mourning like a childless crone
With her sorrow left alone—
The eternal human cry
To the heedless passer-by.

I have said above that Mr. Carman has had three distinct periods, and intimated that the poems in the following collection are of his third period. The first period may be said to be represented by the Low Tide and Behind the Arras volumes, while the second is displayed in the three volumes of Songs from Vagabondia, which he published in association with his friend Richard Hovey. Bliss Carman was from the first too original and individual a poet to be directly influenced by anyone else; but there can be no doubt that his friendship with Hovey helped to turn him from over-preoccupation with mysteries which, for all their greatness, are not for man to solve, to an intenser realisation of the beauty and loveliness of the world about him and of the joys of human fellowship. The result is seen in such poems as "Spring Song," quoted in part above, and his perhaps equally well-known "The Joys of the Road," which appeared in the same volume with that poem, and a few verses from which follow:

Now the joys of the road are chiefly these:
A crimson touch on the hardwood trees;

A vagrant's morning wide and blue,
In early fall, when the wind walks, too;

A shadowy highway cool and brown,
Alluring up and enticing down

From rippled waters and dappled swamp,
From purple glory to scarlet pomp;

The outward eye, the quiet will,
And the striding heart from hill to hill.

Some of the finest of arman's work is contained in his elegiac or memorial poems, in which he commemorates Keats, Shelley, William Blake, Lincoln, Stevenson, and other men for whom he has a kindred feeling, and also friends whom he has loved and lost. Listen to these moving lines from "Non Omnis Moriar," written in memory of Gleeson White, and to be found in Last Songs from Vagabondia:

There is a part of me that knows,
Beneath incertitude and fear,
I shall not perish when I pass
Beyond mortality's frontier;

But greatly having joyed and grieved,
Greatly content, shall hear the sigh

Of the strange wind across the lone
Bright lands of taciturnity.

In patience therefore I await
My friend's unchanged benign regard,—
Some April when I too shall be
Spilt water from a broken shard.

In "The White Gull," written for the centenary of the birth of Shelley in 1892, and included in By the
Aurelian Wall, he thus apostrophizes that clear and shining spirit:

O captain of the rebel host,
Lead forth and far!
Thy toiling troopers of the night
Press on the unavailing fight;
The sombre field is not yet lost,
With thee for star.

Thy lips have set the hail and haste
Of clarions free
To bugle down the wintry verge
Of time forever, where the surge
Thunders and trembles on a waste
And open sea.

In "A Seamark," a threnody for Robert Louis Stevenson, which appears in the same volume, the poet
hails "R.L.S." (of whose tribe he may be said to be truly one) as

The master of the roving kind,

and goes on:

O all you hearts about the world
In whom the truant gypsy blood,
Under the frost of this pale time,
Sleeps like the daring sap and flood
That dreams of April and reprieve!
You whom the haunted vision drives,
Incredulous of home and ease.
Perfection's lovers all your lives!

You whom the wander-spirit loves
To lead by some forgotten clue
Forever vanishing beyond
Horizon brinks forever new;
Our restless loved adventurer,
On secret orders come to him,
Has slipped his cable, cleared the reef,

And melted on the white sea-rim.

"Perfection's lovers all your lives." Of these, it may be said without qualification, is Bliss Carman himself.

No summary of Mr. Carman's work, however cursory, would be worthy of the name if it omitted mention of his ventures in the realm of Greek myth. From the Book of Myths is made up of work of that sort, every poem in it being full of the beauty of phrase and melody of which Mr. Carman alone has the secret. The finest poems in the book, barring the opening one, "Overlord," are "Daphne," "The Dead Faun," "Hylas," and "At Phædra's Tomb," but I can do no more here than name them, for extracts would fail to reveal their full beauty. And beauty, after all is said, is the first and last thing with Mr. Carman. As he says himself somewhere:

The joy of the hand that hews for beauty
Is the dearest solace under the sun.

And again

The eternal slaves of beauty
Are the masters of the world.

A slave—a happy, willing slave—to beauty is the poet himself, and the world can never repay him for the message of beauty which he has brought it.

Kindred to From the Book of Myths, but much more important, is Sappho: One Hundred Lyrics, one of the most successful of the numerous attempts which have been made to recapture the poems by that high priestess of song which remain to us only in fragments. Mr. Carman, as Charles G. D. Roberts points out in an introduction to the volume, has made no attempt here at translation or paraphrasing; his venture has been "the most perilous and most alluring in the whole field of poetry"—that of imaginative and, at the same time, interpretive construction. Brief quotation again would fail to convey an adequate idea of the exquisiteness of the work, and all I can do, therefore, is to urge all lovers of real poetry to possess themselves of Sappho: One Hundred Lyrics, for it is literally a storehouse of lyric beauty.

I must not fail here to speak of From the Book of Valentines, which contains some lovely things, notably "At the Great Release." This is not only one of the finest of all Mr. Carman's poems, but it is also one of the finest poems of our time. It is a love poem, and no one possessing any real feeling for poetry can read it without experiencing that strange thrill of the spirit which only the highest form of poetry can communicate. "Morning and Evening," "In an Iris Meadow," and "A letter from Lesbos" must be also mentioned. In the last named poem, Sappho is represented as writing to Gorgo, and expresses herself in these moving words:

If the high gods in that triumphant time
Have calendared no day for thee to come
Light-hearted to this doorway as of old,
Unmoved I shall behold their pomps go by—
The painted seasons in their pageantry,
The silvery progressions of the moon,
And all their infinite ardors unsubdued,

Pass with the wind replenishing the earth

Incredulous forever I must live
And, once thy lover, without joy behold,
The gradual uncounted years go by,
Sharing the bitterness of all things made.

Mention must be now made of Songs of the Sea Children, which can be described only as a collection of the sweetest and tenderest love lyrics written in our time—

—the lyric songs
The earthborn children sing,
When wild-wood laughter throngs
The shy bird-throats of spring;
When there's not a joy of the heart
But flies like a flag unfurled,
And the swelling buds bring back
The April of the world.

So perfect and complete are these lyrics that it would be almost sacrilege to quote any of them unless entire. Listen however, to these verses:

The day is lost without thee,
The night has not a star.
Thy going is an empty room
Whose door is left ajar.

Depart: it is the footfall
Of twilight on the hills.
Return: and every rood of ground
Breaks into daffodils.

There are those who will have it that Bliss Carman has been away from Canada so long that he has ceased to be, in a real sense, a Canadian. Such assume rather than know, for a very little study of his work would show them that it is shot through and through with the poet's feeling for the land of his birth. Memories of his childhood and youthful years down by the sea are still fresh in Mr. Carman's mind, and inspire him again and again in his writing. "A Remembrance," at the beginning of the present collection, may be pointed to as a striking instance of this, but proof positive is the volume, Songs from a Northern Garden, for it could have been written only by a Canadian, born and bred, one whose heart and soul thrill to the thought of Canada. I would single out from this volume for special mention as being "Canadian" in the fullest sense "In a Grand Pré Garden," "The Keeper's Silence," "At Home and Abroad," "Killoleet," and "Above the Gaspereau," but have no space to quote from them.

But Mr. Carman is not only a Canadian, he is also a Briton; and evidence of this is his Ode on the Coronation, written on the occasion of the crowning of King Edward VII in 1902. This poem—the very existence of which is hardly known among us—ought to be put in the hands of every child and youth who speaks the English tongue, for no other, I dare maintain—nothing by Kipling, or Newbolt, or any other of our so-called "Imperial singers"—expresses more truly and more movingly the deep feeling of love and reverence which the very thought of England evokes in every son of hers, even though it may never have been his to see her white cliffs rise or to tread her storied ground:

O England, little mother by the sleepless Northern tide,
Having bred so many nations to devotion, trust, and pride,
Very tenderly we turn
With welling hearts that yearn
Still to love you and defend you,—let the sons of men discern
Wherein your right and title, might and majesty, reside.

In concluding this, I greatly fear, lamentably inadequate study, I come to the collection which follows, and which, as intimated above, represents the work of Mr. Carman's latest period. I must say at once that, while I yield to no one in admiration for Low Tide and the other books of that period, or for the work of the second period, as represented by the Songs from Vagabondia volumes, I have no hesitation in declaring that I regard the poet's work of the past few years with even higher admiration. It may not possess the force and vigor of the work which preceded it; but anything seemingly missing in that respect is more than made up for me by increased beauty and clarity of expression. The mysticism—verging, or more than verging, at times on symbolism—which marked his earlier poems, and which hung, as it were, as a veil between them and the reader, has gone, and the poet's thought or theme now lies clearly before us as in a mirror. What—to take a verse from the following pages at random—could be more pellucid, more crystal clear in expression—what indeed, could come closer to that achieving of the impossible at which every real poet must aim—than this from "In Gold Lacquer".

Gold are the great trees overhead,
And gold the leaf-strewn grass,
As though a cloth of gold were spread
To let a seraph pass.
And where the pageant should go by,
Meadow and wood and stream,
The world is all of lacquered gold,
Expectant as a dream.

The poet, happily, has fully recovered from the serious illness which laid him low some two years ago, and which for a time caused his friends and admirers the gravest concern, and so we may look forward hopefully to seeing further volumes of verse come from the press to make certain his name and fame. But if, for any reason, this should not be—which the gods forfend!—Later Poems, I dare affirm, must and will be regarded as the fine flower and crowning achievement of the genius and art of Bliss Carman.

R. H. HATHAWAY.
Toronto, 1921.

Bliss Carman – A Short Biography

William Bliss Carman was born in Fredericton, in New Brunswick on April 15th 1861. 'Bliss' was his mother's maiden name. She was descended from Daniel Bliss of Concord, Massachusetts, who was the great-grandfather to Ralph Waldo Emerson.

Carman was educated at Fredericton Collegiate School. Here, under the influence of the headmaster George Robert Parkin, he gained an appreciation of classical literature and was introduced to the poetry of many of the Pre-Raphaelites especially Dante Gabriel Rossetti and Algernon Charles Swinburne.

From here he graduated to the University of New Brunswick, obtaining his B.A. there in 1881. As is common with so many writers his first published piece was for the University magazine and for Carman that was in 1879.

England now beckoned and he spent a year at Oxford and then the University of Edinburgh (1882–1883). He returned home to Canada to work on his M.A. which he obtained from the University of New Brunswick in 1884.

Tragically his father died in January, 1885, followed by his mother in February of the following year. Carman now enrolled in Harvard University for a year. There he met and was part of a literary circle that included the American poet Richard Hovey, who would become his close friend, and later collaborator, on the successful Vagabondia poetry series. Carman and Hovey were members of the "Visionists" circle along with Herbert Copeland and F. Holland Day, who would later form the Boston publishing firm Copeland & Day and, in turn, launch Vagabondia.

After Harvard Carman briefly returned to Canada, but was back in Boston by February of 1890 saying "Boston is one of the few places where my critical education and tastes could be of any use to me in earning money. New York and London are about the only other places." However, he was unable to find work in Boston but was more successful in New York becoming the literary editor of the semi-religious New York Independent. There he helped Canadian poets get published and introduced them to a wider readership than they could receive in Canada.

However, Carman and work as an editor were not destined for a long career together and he was dismissed in 1892. There followed short stays with Current Literature, Cosmopolitan, The Chap-Book, and The Atlantic Monthly. Whilst these appointments provided the basis for a career and an income he was not suited to their demands. From 1895 he would only work as a contributor to magazines and newspapers whilst he worked on his volumes of poetry.

Carman first published a book of poetry in 1893 with Low Tide on Grand Pré. He had written the title poem in the summer of 1886 and it had (whilst he was still at Harvard) been published in the spring of 1887 by Atlantic Monthly. Despite its critical acceptance there was no Canadian company prepared to publish the volume. When an American company did so it went bankrupt. Life was becoming difficult for the young poet.

The following year was decidedly better. His partnership with Richard Hovey had given birth to Songs of Vagabondia and it was published by their friends at Copeland & Day. It was an immediate success. The young men were delighted at such a reception. It quickly sold out and was re-printed a number of times. Although these re-prints were small (usually 500-1000 copies) they were frequent.

On the back of this success they would write a further three volumes, which in their turn were almost as successful. They quickly became the center of a cult following, especially among students who empathized with the poetry's anti-materialistic themes, its celebration of personal freedom, and its glorification of comradeship."

The success of Songs of Vagabondia prompted the Boston firm, Stone & Kimball, to reissue Low Tide on Grand Pré and to hire Carman as the editor of its literary journal, The Chapbook. This ceased after a year when the company relocated and Carman expressed his desire to remain in Boston.

In 1885 Carman brought out Behind the Arras, a somewhat more serious and philosophical work centered on the premise of a long meditation using the speaker's house and its many rooms as a symbol of life and the choices to be made. However, the idea and its execution did not quite meld.

Signficantly, in 1896, Carman met Mrs Mary Perry King, who rapidly became patron, adviser and sometime lover. She put money in his pocket, and food in his mouth and, when he struck bottom, often repaired his confidence as well as helping to sell the work. She also later became his writing collaborator on two verse dramas.

Mitchell Kennerley, Carman's roommate wrote that, "On the rare occasions they had intimate relations they always advised me of by leaving a bunch of violets — Mary favorite flower — on the pillow of my bed." If her husband, Dr. King, knew of this arrangement he seems not to have objected. He was a great supporter of Carman's career and seemingly his wife's complicated involvement with that.

In 1897 Carman published Ballad of Lost Haven, a collection of poetry about the sea. Its notable poems include the macabre sea shanty, The Gravedigger. The following year, 1898, came By the Aurelian Wall, the title poem itself was an elegy to John Keats and the book a collection of formal elegies.

In 1899 his publisher, Lamson, Wolffe was taken over by the Boston firm of Small, Maynard & Co., who had also acquired the rights to Low Tide on Grand Pré. The copyrights to of his books were now held by one publisher and, in lieu of earnings, Carman took what would ultimately be a disastrous financial stake in the company.

As the century turned Carman was hard at work on what would eventually be a five-volume set of poetry; "Pans Pipes". Pan, the goat-god, was traditionally associated with poetry and the coming together of the earthly and the divine. The five volumes were all published between 1902 – 1905.

The inspiration for this came from Mary who had persuaded Carman to write in both prose and poetry about the ideas of 'unitrinianism.' This drew on the theories of François-Alexandre-Nicolas-Chéri Delsarte and was defined as a strategy of mind-body-spirit harmonization aimed at undoing the physical, psychological, and spiritual damage caused by urban modernity. The definition may be rather woolly but for Carman it resulted in some very fine work across the five-volume series. This shared belief between Mary and Carman created a further bond but did isolate him from his circle of friends.

The excellence of a number of these poems did much to install Carman as the most noted of Canadian Poets and eventually their own Poet Laureate. Among the most often quoted and printed are "The Dead Faun" (from Volume I), "Lord of My Heart's Elation" (Volume II) and many of the erotic poems from Volume III.

In the middle of publication in 1903, Small, Maynard failed and with it went all the assets Carman had tied up in the company.

Carman immediately signed with another Boston publisher, L.C. Page, who would publish seven new books of Carman poetry in this hectic period up to 1905. They released a further three books based on Carman's Transcript columns, and a prose work on Unitrinianism, The Making of Personality, that he'd written with Mary King.

Carman now felt secure enough to pursue his 'dream project,' namely a deluxe edition of his collected poetry to 1903. Page acquired the distribution rights on the condition that the book be sold privately, by subscription. Unfortunately, the demand wasn't there and it failed. Carman was deeply disappointed and lost faith in Page. However, their grip on his copyrights was absolute and sadly no further collected editions were to be published during his lifetime.

By 1904 his income was restricted and the offer to be editor-in-chief of the 10-volume project, The World's Best Poetry, was eagerly accepted.

For Carman perhaps his best years as a poet were now behind him. From 1908 he lived near the Kings' New Canaan, Connecticut, estate, that he named "Sunshine", or in the summer in a cabin in the Catskills, which he called "Moonshine."

With Literary tastes now moving away from what he could provide his income further dwindled and his health started to deteriorate.

In 1912 Carman published the final work in the Vagabondia series. Richard Hovey had died in 1900 and so this last work was purely his. It has a distinct elegiac tone as if remembering the past works themselves.

Although Carman was not politically active he did campaign during the World War One, as a member of the Vigilantes, who supported the American entry into the titanic struggle on the Allied side.

By 1920, Carman was impoverished and recovering from a near-fatal attack of tuberculosis. He returned to Canada and began to undertake a series of publicly successful and somewhat lucrative reading tours, saying "there is nothing worth talking of in book sales compared with reading. Breathless attention, crowded halls, and a strange, profound enthusiasm such as I never guessed could be,' he reported to a friend. 'And good thrifty money too. Think of it! An entirely new life for me, and I am the most surprised person in Canada.'"

On October 28th, 1921 Carman was honored at a dinner held by the newly-formed Canadian Authors' Association, at the Ritz Carlton Hotel in Montreal, where he was crowned Canada's Poet Laureate with a wreath of maple leaves.

Carman is placed among the Confederation Poets, a group that included his cousin, Charles G.D. Roberts, Archibald Lampman, and Duncan Campbell Scott. Carman was perhaps the best and is credited with the widest recognition. However, whilst the others carefully supplemented their income with writing novels and works for the magazines, or even other careers, Carman only wrote poetry together with a small amount of writing on literary ideas, philosophy, and aesthetics.

He continued his reading tours, and by 1925 had finally secured a new Canadian publisher; McClelland & Stewart (Toronto), who issued a collection of selected earlier verse and would now became his main publisher. Although they benefited from Carman's increased popularity and his revered position in

Canadian literature, his former publisher L.C. Page would not relinquish its copyrights to his earlier works.

In his last years, Carman was a member of the Halifax literary and social set, The Song Fishermen and in 1927 he edited The Oxford Book of American Verse.

William Bliss Carman died of a brain hemorrhage, at the age of 68, in New Canaan on the 8th June, 1929. He was cremated in New Canaan and his ashes interred at Forest Hill Cemetery, Fredericton, with a national memorial service held at the Anglican cathedral there.

It was only a quarter of a century later, on May 13th, 1954, that a scarlet maple tree was planted at his graveside, to honour his request in the 1892 poem "The Grave-Tree":

Let me have a scarlet maple
For the grave-tree at my head,
With the quiet sun behind it,
In the years when I am dead.

Bliss Carman – A Concise Bibliography

Poetry Collections
Low Tide on Grand Pre: A Book of Lyrics (1893)
Songs from Vagabondia (1894)
A Seamark: A Threnody for Robert Louis Stevenson (1895)
Behind the Arras: A Book of the Unseen (1895)
More Songs from Vagabondia (1896)
Ballads of Lost Haven: A Book of the Sea (1897)
By the Aurelian Wall: And Other Elegies (1898)
A Winter Holiday (1899)
Last Songs from Vagabondia (1901)
Ballads and Lyrics (1902)
Ode on the Coronation of King Edward (1902)
Pipes of Pan: From the Book of Myths (1902)
Pipes of Pan: From the Green Book of the Bards (1903)
Pipes of Pan: Songs of the Sea Children (1904)
Pipes of Pan: Songs from a Northern Garden (1904)
Pipes of Pan: From the Book of Valentines (1905)
Sappho: One Hundred Lyrics (1904)
Poems (1905)
The Rough Rider: And Other Poems (1909)
A Painter's Holiday, and Other Poems (1911)
Echoes from Vagabondia (1912)
April Airs: A Book of New England Lyrics (1916)
The Man of The Marne: And Other Poems (1918)
The Vengeance of Noel Brassard: A Tale of the Acadian Expulsion (1919)
Far Horizons (1925)

Later Poems (1926)
Sanctuary: Sunshine House Sonnets (1929)
Wild Garden (1929)
Bliss Carman's Poems (1931)

Drama
Bliss Carman & Mary Perry King. Daughters of Dawn: A Lyrical Pageant of a Series of Historical Scenes for Presentation with Music and Dancing (1913)
Bliss Carman & Mary Perry King. Earth Deities: And Other Rhythmic Masques (1914)

Prose Collections
The Kinship of Nature (1904)
The Poetry of Life (1905)
The Friendship of Art (1908)
The Making of Personality (1908)
Talks on Poetry and Life; Being a Series of Five Lectures Delivered Before the University of Toronto, December 1925 (Speech). transcribed by Blanche Hume. 1926.
Bliss Carman's Scrap-Book: A Table of Contents (Pierce, Lorne, editor) (1931)

Editor
The World's Best Poetry (10 volumes) (1904)
The Oxford Book of American Verse (U.S. editor) (1927)
Carman, Bliss; Pierce, Lorne, editors (1935). Our Canadian Literature: Representative Verse, English and French.

www.ingramcontent.com/pod-product-compliance
Lightning Source LLC
Chambersburg PA
CBHW060049050426
42448CB00011B/2364